GOD HATES DIVORCE

Malachi 2:16

A Wife's Guide to a Successful Marriage
The Heavenly Marriage Series
Volume One

BETTIE J. RUSHER

Scribes of Eden Publishing
Detroit   Atlanta
www.scribesofeden.com

ISBN: 978-0-9985555-0-8

Printed in the United States of America

Go to website to download Free E-book,
My Go To Scriptures
www.backtoeden.today

Dedication

I dedicate my life and this book, **God Hates Divorce** to the Almighty GOD, who created me for such a time as this. My daily prayer is that I would live a life that brings my Heavenly Father glory. The Heavenly Marriage Series was on GOD's Agenda long before I showed up; therefore, I am sure that it will be used as He sees fit.

Just a vessel,

Bettie J Rusher

Table of Contents

What the Wives are Saying

"This book will transform how you view marriage and ultimately how you live your life. It will teach you how to be the virtuous wife that God has called you to be while strengthening your reliance on the Most High God. Thank God for the vision and shared knowledge of this author."

Remy C. Woods

"I thought it was all HIM! Surely it couldn't be me after all I was doing everything right! What a shock to read and have an understanding...that BABY, I was coming up short! I hadn't done half the things I could have done to make it better. I am a witness that if you apply these practices, you will see a fresh dose of LOVE take over! It's been so sweet and so good to me! I'm thankful and grateful for this book, it has given me new hope in my relationship!"

C. Austin

"*God Hates Divorce*, this marriage-life book is one of the most realistic books that I've had the honor to read. It will make you laugh, cry, change, and pray all at the same time. LOL! Mrs. Bettie Rusher has guided me through marital issues (separation) using some of these same scriptures within this book that has restored my marriage. Allow it to make an impact in your life as well."

Mrs. Corgial

Forward

The Heavenly Marriage Series
Volume 1

This book is a guide written with my blood, sweat, and tears for ALL women. You will find pertinent insight to aid unmarried women in the preparation and/or contemplating stage, the new bride, the wife that's in a smooth sailing stage, the wife in the OMG (Oh, My God) stage, the champion wife that's in the midst of active battle, and for the seasoned, mature wife to serve as a reminder to keep your hands on the plow… to never get distracted or be deceived that you got it all together.

Excerpts from My Memoirs

The Diary of a Virtuous Woman.

16 days before our 21st Wedding Anniversary

A day that I will not forget. After 20+ years of marriage, my husband announced that he planned to file for divorce by the end of the week and that he was moving out soon. We were sitting in his office when he said those life choking words to me. I instantly felt a warm rush from my head to my toes in slow motion. I slumped down in my seat and released a moan; I am sure he thought I was in shock or grief. Strangely enough, I was not, I actually felt comforted. I responded by asking him when he planned to leave. I didn't say anything else, I just retreated to our bedroom, my sanctuary.

I fell to the floor on my face and began to pray. God reminded me that some years ago, He revealed to me that I would write a book entitled, <u>God Hates Divorce</u>. I guessed this would be a good time to put my thoughts on paper.

Our 21st Wedding Anniversary

I woke up to a very still and cold house. No balloons or flowers, not even a whispered Happy Anniversary. Disheartened, I went for a walk, upon returning home, I spotted his cell phone on the table. Lately, I had become an in-house private detective. There was the evidence; he had talked with her twice already! Ok, Bettie, what do you do with this information? All day, it festered inside of me. His stubborn silence didn't help to ease my pain. Finally, I exploded!! He apologized again for the continual infidelity, took his wedding ring off, placed it gently on the table and said he would return the next day for his belongings. Wow!! *Happy 21st Anniversary!!*

Allow the words of my song to resound loud and clear...

YES, HE DID

"He Left Me for Another Woman, Yes, He Did,
On Our 21st Wedding Anniversary Day!

No, He Didn't, Yes, He Did!!
But God Kept Me from Doing Prison Time. Yes, My God Kept My Mind and Made Me Whole!

Yes, HE Did!

I will share other excerpts as we continue to add to the saga; watch out for the forthcoming edition of the <u>Diary of the Victorious Wife</u>. The best is yet to come!

Introduction

GOD HATES DIVORCE!
The Heavenly Marriage Series
Volume 1

This book is 31 chapters of my journey; I share Warfare Strategies, Prayers, and Confessions that I obtained and practiced during the good times and not so good times. During seasons of intense warfare, I literally had to kick Satan out of my marriage and home. He tried every tactic to get me to run and abandon my home and marriage BUT GOD said: "THERE WILL BE NO DIVORCE!" That meant that I had to learn how to stand and gain the courage to not run. God said, "He will teach our hands to fight." God fought the battle; all I had to do was come into agreement with His will and use the following strategies, prayers and confessions daily. Don't think I'm crazy; I could actually see the devil's shadow in my foyer at the foot of my staircase standing with his arms crossed, with a stance as if he was planted with no plans to leave. At first, I was afraid, but as days went by, I got stronger in the Lord and in the Power of His Might. I began to say, "You are leaving here!" It was a tumultuous battle for months, he didn't leave right away. Yes, there was a door that was opened to allow him access; therefore, I must continue to live by these disciplines because Satan hasn't given up and would love to take my testimony of defeating the demon of adultery and now experiencing a Heavenly Marriage!

Standing Up for Your Marriage is a Lifestyle and Will Require Work!

Everyone desires a Heavenly Marriage but are you willing to do what it takes behind closed doors, in your prayer closet to have and maintain one? I was advised by the clergy, marriage counselors, and others to give up on our marriage before I lost my mind. My family and friends were lovingly concerned when I had lost over 40 pounds, I was literally skin and bones. I was admonished to ignore God, surely, He didn't want me to suffer like this. Therefore, I became rather recluse during this dark season, only talking to a few loved ones, and desperately resorting to books, but mainly to the Bible to seek His Wisdom, Knowledge, and Understanding.

Hopefully, you will begin to live and breathe God's Living Word found in this volume to kick and/or keep the devil out of your marriage. I pray that these words will equip you, that you may avoid pain and unhappiness. However; I don't regret the suffering I endured because it prepared me to write to you today. I can truly tell you that whatever you are going through and regardless of how it looks, God can fix it. I am a true witness that there is Abundant Life even after Adultery and Brokenness that may come in any form.

Start by daily confessing these words:
I Am Heavenly Married, Yes I am!!

Download 1: You Said, "I Do!"

Did you read the fine print?

"And the Lord God said, "It is not good that man should be alone; I will make him a helper comparable to him."
Genesis 2:18 NKJV

Queen, tell the truth, how many days out of the last 365 have you prayed for your husband? Wow, 365 days, that's great! But for those of you who, like me, may have come up a little short, I wonder what happened on the days that you missed praying? Perhaps, his mom, sister, grandmother or pastor had his back and prayed for him, maybe not. The reality is that you are the only person with the spiritual obligation to pray for *your* husband. After all, he has left his mother and father to cleave to you, right?

Men often don't pray for themselves until their backs are against the wall and then it becomes a Prayer of

Desperation. Why is it human nature to wait until things are desperate before most really pray?

Your husband urgently needs your prayers *every day*! That's seven days a week, not Monday through Friday and off on weekends. There may have been days, weeks, even months that *absolutely no one has prayed for your husband*! No wonder he acts the way he does. He is weary, frustrated, confused, and stagnated because of the never-ending warfare that the enemy is waging against him. He feels as if he is fighting a lost battle. The devil wants to keep *your* husband bound.

My Sister, make a commitment to God and *your* husband to *stop complaining and pray* each and every day for him. Be aware that there is an increase in demonic activity especially during the summer months. That is definitely not the time to slack off, but increase the intensity of prayer. Those of you who have this discipline, you know the results of consistent prayer and the benefits of not getting weary in so doing. Now is the time to barrage the kingdom of darkness on behalf of your husband and family!

Let Us Pray

Father, first of all, I repent for the days that I neglected to pray for my husband. Thank You for Your faithfulness to us even when we have been unfaithful. Help me to develop a habit of diligently praying for Your son. I realize that we need to recover the territory that may have been lost due to my ignorance, inconsistency or neglect. I realize that he needs me to do so. On this week, please honor my effort. In Jesus' mighty name, amen!

Our Confession

I'm forgiven for my lack of diligence in praying for *my* husband. I count it as a privilege and accept the responsibility to pray daily for him. He is getting stronger in every area each and every day.

I Am Heavenly Married; Yes, I Am!!

Download 2: Make Up For Lost Time!

Don't attempt to understand, just do it!

"Making the very most of your time [on earth, recognizing and taking advantage of each opportunity and using it with wisdom and diligence], because the days are filled with evil."
Ephesians 5:16 Amplified Bible

Sister, on this week, begin today to call out your husband's name to God, at least, ten times each day. I found that when I called out my husband's name something supernatural begins to happen, and I can't stop there, but continued to pray for him. It got so good that sometimes, I called out his full name; I wanted to make sure God knew exactly who I was talking about.

Let Us Pray

Heavenly Father, thank You for allowing me to redeem and make up for the opportunities that I missed praying for Your son. As I fervently call out his name to You this week, please place the love that You have for my husband deeper and deeper into my heart. Allow him to feel the intensity of my prayers as never before. I understand that Jesus is praying for him, therefore; I come into total agreement with Jesus' prayers for him. I thank You for a supernatural week of redeeming the time that was lost. Thank You, Jesus. Amen!

Our Confession

I will continually call out *my* husband's name to God. God knows his name and God's glory is on him. The love that is in my heart for him is expanding day by day!

I Am Heavenly Married; Yes, I Am!!

Download 3:
God Has A Heavenly Plan!

The beginning of a new life.

"That is why a man will leave
his father and mother.
He marries a woman, and the two of them become one person."
Genesis 2:24 Contemporary English Version

Sis, how does God make two people one? The process starts before your wedding day. Perhaps, while both of you were in your mom's womb! Do you recall how challenging it was to come together? Were you Bridezilla? You wanted one thing and he wanted something entirely different. Somehow you both worked it out! That was the beginning of the process. Now, here you are, and maybe you don't see eye to eye. One may seem to be moving faster and in opposition to the other. He seems to not want to grow up and change. Or is it you that is fighting the process?

I believe that oneness is truly possible, even if it takes a lifetime. God is patiently molding both of you into a beautiful work of art. I can see you now, a beautiful masterpiece that He is so proud of; a trophy that God can put on display, *Mr. and Mrs.*! He loves to take you to places to show you off. The world has been waiting to behold your radiance. This is magnificent, a miracle, two individuals who are one in God's sight.

Let Us Pray

Father, I come to You in Jesus' name realizing that You are creating a masterpiece, an original. Help me not to look at other marriages and compare because You are creating a unique and awesome marriage between my husband and me. Help me to be patient with him knowing that we are a work in progress. I look forward to the impact our marriage will have on the world as they behold Your glory in our lives. Father, use our marriage to win souls. Humbly, we pray. Amen.

Our Confession

Our marriage wins souls and brings God's glory! I am one with *my* husband. My being in submission to him is a joy.

I Am Heavenly Married; Yes, I Am!!

Download 4:
Wash Your Mouth!

**Your words will come back to
bless or haunt you.**

*"Life and Death is in the power of
your tongue."*
Proverbs 18:21

Queen, have you ever been surprised by the words that come out of your mouth? You may have thought, where did that come from? Maybe, it wasn't what you said, but the tone was surprising. Or he rubbed you the wrong way and you had a cursing fit. I know, the devil made you do it! Washing your mouth with soap would be deserved punishment! I'm joking, LOL!

Sometimes, I'm short-tempered and just plain cranky with my husband; especially when he bombards me with so many questions. I listened to myself the other day and thought, *I could have said that in a kinder way.* I have also been known to ignore his questions rather than speak with an edge which is wrong and disrespectful.

My role model is in the Bible; the Virtuous Wife. Proverbs 31 verse 2 states, "*she opens her mouth with wisdom and in her tongue, is the law of kindness.*" Sis, please help me, what is the law of kindness? It sounds like something that I need.

Then I ran across this, "Do not let any unwholesome talk come out of your mouth, but only what is helpful for building others up according to their need; that it may benefit those who listen." Ephesians 4:29.

Now, that is the litmus test...*If my words benefit the person who I am talking to, I will pass!* Yes, it may have been the truth but could I've said it in a kinder way?

When we fail the test, we need to check our hearts. Sometimes, it is not that deep, perhaps just being tired. Be quick to apologize, end the discussion and simply go to bed! Start over the next day, it is amazing what a good night rest can do.

Other times, we really need to take our attitudes to the altar, because something is going on inside. Seriously, those slip ups, verbal fits, and funky fragrances need to be checked in, "Oh, well," won't do.

After all, we are being forewarned that at the end of the day. "*...every idle (careless) word men speak; they will give account of it in the Day of Judgment.*" Matthew 12:36.

Ouch! Have mercy, Lord!

Let Us Pray

Father, Father, Father, HELP! Forgive me for dishonoring my husband with my words and attitudes. Help me to live out Your Word in James 1:19 "to be slow to speak, slow to anger and quick to listen." I understand the power of my words. I desire to build up my husband with kind words. I confess any known bitterness in my heart because it hinders our oneness. Father, if there is any unknown sin in my heart, please reveal it. Use my mouth to speak Your will into Your son's life. My words will create and glorify You, O God. I pray in Jesus' name. Amen.

Our Confession

I am slow to speak, slow to anger and quick to listen. My husband loves to hear my voice of encouragement, love and words of faith. Our hearts have been washed in the Blood of Jesus, and we walk in forgiveness every day. I strive not to bring up any brokenness of our past. We are free!

I Am Heavenly Married; Yes, I Am!!

Download 5: Invaluable Meek And Quiet Spirit!

A Priceless & Rare Gift

> "Ladies, adorn yourself with a meek and quiet spirit
> which is in the sight of God
> of great price."
> 2 Peter 3:4

Well, that settles it; if God says that a meek and quiet spirit is of value, I want and need it! I asked God for a meek and quiet spirit the very day that I understood this scripture. I didn't feel any different, but by faith I believed that I had received this gift that was great in God's eyes.

Sometime ago; my husband and I were having a "discussion" and I was determined to have the last word. I opened my mouth and nothing came out. I was actually thinking what I wanted to express, my lips were actually moving but no sound came out. Then I remembered my prayer and also at the same time, realized that the words that I wanted to say were harmful.

Oh, my God. Life has been different for me ever since and that has been many years ago. When people ask my husband, what does your wife do when she is upset? He will reply, she usually goes to our bedroom (my sanctuary) and read. What would be your husband's answer? It is wise to provide yourself a place to calm down and regroup. It will allow God the opportunity to speak to both of your hearts. Giving each other distance can make an everlasting difference.

I have found that this quiet and meek spirit also displays great strength.

Let Us Pray

Father, thank you for this meek and quiet spirit which you said is of great price. I am honored to possess it with my whole heart. Help my husband to honor this gift that you have given me and not to take advantage of it. Make him to recognize that my meekness and quietness is a strength and not a weakness. Thank You for speaking to both of us during those times of quietness. Condition our ears to hear Your voice. Continue to shut my mouth that he will hear Your voice and not mine. In Jesus' Name, Amen!

Our Confession

I possess a meek and quiet spirit. I am slow to speak, slow to anger and quick to listen. My godly behavior has won my husband. I am respected and honored by him and our children!

I Am Heavenly Married, Yes, I Am!!

Download 6:
Each Day Is A New Day!

A lifetime commitment.

"...Forgetting those things which are behind, and reaching forward to those things which are ahead. I press towards the goal for the prize of the upward call of God in Christ Jesus."
Philippians 3:13-14

GET THE PRIZE! These are the words that I heard one morning when I was struggling to cook breakfast for my husband. To be exact, *"Bettie, get the prize."* It was a personal, quiet and gentle push. I thought about the above scripture: I suddenly got excited and the drudgery disappeared. I remembered that the above scripture emphasized pressing past that uncomfortable place. Guess, what I did? I pressed and proceeded to throw pots and pans on the stove. My husband started his day with a meal fit for a king. Thanks, be to God.

Queen, as you continue to pray for your husband, seven days each week, there will be days you won't feel like it. Press in, and remember the prize. Great victories are won on the days when your flesh doesn't want to cooperate.

Please note: The days when he is everything but the perfect husband and it is hard to even look at him, are the days that your husband *really needs you to pray.*

Sister, remember each time that it is a press and you do it anyway, the enemy is defeated!

Let Us Pray

Father, I need strength to be consistent and press to pray when my mind and body doesn't want to. I desire to be mindful that my husband needs me to pray every day. Allow me to see answers to my prayers quickly. Thank You for this new love that I possess to protect and minister to my husband in this special way. As I pray for him; I can discern someone is praying for me too. Thank You, Father, that Your ways are so much higher and different than ours. I agree with Jesus' prayer today, Amen.

Our Confession

I press every day to execute my assignment. I draw from Your strength as I humbly depend on You for my existence. I can't do anything without You, but can do all things with Your help. I am more than a conqueror and possess all that my husband needs his wife to be!

I Am Heavenly Married; Yes, I Am!!

Download 7:
A Mountain Moving Smile!

Looking in the mirror and give yourself a big smile every day.

*"A glad heart makes a happy face;
a broken heart crushes the spirit."*
Proverbs 15.13

My Sister, you have a God-given power, to make him sweat with emotion! You can move a mountain with your smile.

Smiling is a facial expression of inward emotion. Sometimes, husbands will attempt to hide the fact that you just blessed them and refuse to smile. They will tend to blush, turn their heads or have a poker faces so you won't know that you created some pleasure, affection, and happiness. No problem, you must continue to smile until that mountain moves.

This week, put aside your differences and create some inward motion! Discover new ways to make *your* husband smile!

Back in the days, as a Lady of the Night, I developed and practiced skills to make a man smile. The more skillful I became, the more money I made. I found that married men were the neediest. I wondered why?

Now, I know...some wives are experts and specialize in making their man frown, growl, and cry; and are proud of it. Of course, I am not talking about you.

I love to see my husband smile; at times his eyes light up and his face radiates especially when our granddaughter calls him Grandpa. I desire to have that same effect on him.

Remember, other women are devising plans to make your husband smile. It may be a subtle flirt in the form of a look or a kind word. Men need attention. You must stay in the game by keeping your husband engaged. It is never too late to flip the switch; add something new and exciting. Seek advice on how to get his attention again. Be honest with yourself, is he at home physically, but absent in spirit? Is he making excuses for not being home? Does he prefer being with the *guys*? This is just another reality check.

Let Us Pray

Father, I pray that my husband is content in our relationship. Give him the wisdom and strength to handle every flirtatious action. Wash his consciousness of every unclean thought and desire. Thank You for giving him simple joys to make him smile. Help me to be skillful to cause him to smile and light up on the inside. I appreciate positive individuals that come along side of us to make my husband's life pleasant. Thank You for precious memories that will make him smile forever. In Jesus' Name, Amen!

Our Confession

I love to smile. My smile is contagious and moves mountains. I am an expert at causing my husband to smile. When he smiles, the gifts and fruit of the spirit are activated in his life. Your son has a beautiful smile!

I Am Heavenly Married; Yes, I Am!!

Download 8:
Pace Yourself!

Self-Perseverance.

*"But he who endures to the end
shall be saved."*
Matthew 24:13

Wisdom and Knowledge are to be shared! One day, a wise woman stopped me to "chat". She had noticed that I was always running on Fast Forward. I hadn't developed the skill of time management.

She asked me to draw a month calendar on a piece of paper and to write Sabbath on every Sunday. She then asked me to select one day of the week as my sabbath, I chose Monday. I then wrote Bettie's sabbath on every Monday.

That was over 25 years ago, Monday is still my sabbath. I have found that people and situations will put demands on your life 24/7, that is, if you allow it. My family & close associates know that on Mondays, I am usually in cruise mode. They respect my chosen day of rest. Occasionally, I have to switch days but I usually get one in every week or else by Saturday, I can really feel the difference and you may want to avoid me.

Ladies, get a calendar or create one as I did and select a day of sabbath. Put "You" on your calendar; schedule some "Me" time every week. Even, if it is one evening or morning. Be consistent and announce your sabbath day to the world. You may have to fight for it at first, but they will soon respect your desire. *You are important!*

Don't procrastinate, this week, proclaim your sabbath time. Pray about this important decision, this may make the difference of years added to your life, as well as, your well-being.

Sister, on your sabbath day, don't forget to pray for *your* husband.

Let Us Pray

Father, thank You for my sabbath day to be recharged. Help my husband to understand and encourage me as I take time for myself. As I experience the benefit of resting; I will respect the times that Your son wants to be alone. Show me where I can provide a special place in our home for him to relax. Thank You, Jesus, for showing me how important it is to rejuvenate and maintain a slower pace. It's done, Amen!

Our Confession

I appreciate my weekly sabbath. I use this time of rejuvenation to focus on My God. I love our fellowship and look forward to our special time together. Nothing or nobody can come between us, not even His son!

I Am Heavenly Married; Yes, I Am!!

Download 9: He Trusts Me!

It feels good to be needed!

*"The heart of her husband does
trust in her…"*
Proverbs 31:11

This is working! One morning *my* husband came to me while I was sitting at my desk, took my hand as he bent down, placed it on his head and said: *"Pray for me."* Me being nosy, I wanted to ask, "What's wrong?" but God shut my mouth. I calmly allowed the Holy Spirit the opportunity to give me what to pray because He knows.

This week, instead of praying about your husband's shortcomings…try making a list of the things that you love about him, those special traits that make him so uniquely, your honey.

You may have thought, there isn't anything that I love or like about my husband right now. I have been there. The enemy wants us to focus on their faults and overlook the good in them.

Once you have your list, pray to God to enhance those qualities. Throughout the week, show your appreciation by thanking him for some of the things that you often take for granted. When was the last time you said thanks *when he gave you some physical attention*?

Let Us Pray

Father, I am honored to be my husband's personal intercessor! I believe Your word, that when I pray Your will, You hear and answer my prayers. I thank You for the positive changes in our home, regardless of how small. As I look at this list of my husband's strengths, my prayer is that the weaknesses be eliminated. I thank You for my husband's humility to willfully pray with me. I thank You that we are a praying family. In Jesus' Name, I pray, Amen.

Our Confession

I am thankful for my husband. His good qualities by far outnumber his faults. My prayers are being answered every day because I pray according to Your will. I am in agreement with Jesus' Prayers every day!

I Am Heavenly Married; Yes, I Am!!

Download 10:
God Is Laughing With You!

Laugh even when it hurts.

"A merry heart doeth good as a medicine
but a broken spirit dries the bones."
Proverbs 17.22

"Ha, Ha, Ha!! LOL. Ha, Ha!! Whew Wee!!! Ha, Ha!! This is hilarious!! LOL...No, he didn't what? Ha, Ha (while holding my side). Ha, Ha, Ha (with tears in my eyes!) Ok, Ok. Hold up. I need to sit down to catch my breath! O, my God!"

Laughter is the medicine prescribed for you today. Four doses of laughter a day: one dose of laughter this morning, I know that you may not feel it, just do it. Make yourself laugh!! Start with just a he, he, hum.

Then another dose of laughter this afternoon, just think about what your enemy tried to do and how he failed. Ha,

Ha! Ok, you are feeling better already, this self-imposed laughter really works.

Now, it's time for the evening dose of laughter! Have you thought about how far you have come? Reflect on the last 24 hours; how God kept you from dangers seen and unseen.

Whoa, this is different; you are feeling it...light has come into your understanding. You realize that you are victorious and your enemy is defeated, he is a joke, Jesus won the battle for you over 2,000 years ago, the devil is faking it, he knows that he has been stripped, openly cast down and crushed, his game is deception, and one of his tactics is discouragement.

Well, Queen, let's end the day with a final dose of laughter. You are going to confuse the enemy with your heartfelt, from the belly laughter. He will be shocked thinking that you should be somewhere crying, unable to sleep, biting your fingers (not nails), raiding the fridge and the liquor cabinet and close to a nervous breakdown, *but you are unashamedly laughing* at him and his imps!! Your laughter is a weapon that confuses the devil. You must learn to laugh even when it hurts.

Nugget: I have a favorite television show that makes me laugh that helps me get my daily dose. Also, my husband makes me laugh. It is good to spend time with people that make you laugh. The enemy wants to take your laughter away.

The conclusion of the matter: God said, *"He will yet fill your mouth with laughing, and your lips with rejoicing."* Job 8:21

Laughing is contagious. Laugh with your honey tonight.

Let Us Pray

Father, thank You for this revelation regarding self-imposed laughter. Laughter just bubbles up inside of me at the thought of laughing because of the joy within. Again, Your ways are so different than ours. I laugh at every tactic that the enemy has attempted to use against my husband. I thank You that my laughter is filling our home with Your joyous presence. I believe that the laughter is erasing every tear that we have shed. As I'm laughing, my husband is experiencing a supernatural release of stress and the cares of this life are diminishing. Help me to remember this supernatural weapon, whenever we are burdened. Thank You, Father, for teaching me Your ways. Laughing with Jesus, Amen!

Our Confession

Laughter is a part of my daily life. Joy springs up within as I see God's glory in the simplest things. My laughter is contagious and my husband enjoys being in my presence.

He loves to hear me laugh and is touched by its sound. I vow to laugh at his corny jokes!

I Am Heavenly Married; Yes, I Am!!

Download 11:
Heavenly Harmony
And Peace!

There is light at the end of the tunnel.

"How can two walk together
unless they agree?"
Amos 3.3

For years, I prayed for peace with *my* husband, to have a day without an argument was a *miracle*!

God answered my prayer, we no longer argued. It was quiet around the house, we had finally figured out how to co-exist without conflict. We avoided discussing certain topics and learned what buttons not to push. I finally got what I asked for, but something was still missing.

Harmony was the missing element! I always thought that peace and harmony were the same, not quite true. When I think of harmony, I think of music. Visualize an orchestra of thirty instruments making beautiful, melodious sounds that soothe the soul of the hearer. How does that happen? That's supernatural.

You and your husband preparing a meal together or working together daily, to accomplish life goals is beautiful music which comes with harmony.

Queen, people need to see you and your man flowing like this. People long to see this type of interaction between spouses. It is an unusually beautiful sight. Many married couples compromise and settle for the peace in a relationship, but God wants to give us the same harmony that He enjoys with His Son and the Holy Spirit. Your home's atmosphere can be so inviting that people will enjoy visiting and won't want to leave the awesome presence of God in your home. This is the Heavenly Marriage that we desire.

It is required that both you and *your* husband come to an agreement to submit to each other to create this type of lifestyle. It is a daily walk of give and take, compromising and yielding to one another.

Let Us Pray

Father, I pray for the same Oneness that You, Jesus and the Holy Spirit enjoy. I pray that my husband and I come to an understanding that we must submit at times to each other.

I pray that stubbornness and unwillingness to change be removed from us. Allow Your peace and harmony to abide and rule in our home. We thank You that it is contagious and our children are a product of this heavenly environment. We desire a heaven right here on earth. Let Your kingdom come on earth and Your will be done in our home. In Jesus' Name, Amen!

Our Confession

I will strive to walk in heavenly peace with *my* husband daily. I create and maintain harmony and peace in our home. I am the keeper of our home and I will give no place to the enemy. Jesus is Lord of our home all day and every day!

I Am Heavenly Married; Yes, I Am!!

Download 12: Your Home Reflects Your Values!

Woman of the House

"The aged women likewise, that they behave as becomes holiness, not false accusers, not given to much wine, teachers of good things; That they may teach the young women to be sober, to love their husbands, to love their children, to be discreet, chaste, keepers at home, good, obedient to their own husbands that the word of God be not blasphemed (evil spoken of)."

Titus 2.3-5

"God, give me more Patience and Grace today to be the woman that you have called me to be. Thank You!"

This was my prayer one morning as I walked through my home cleaning and washing; cleaning, washing, cleaning, washing…, it is an unending cycle!

So, what did, I do? I decided that the cleaning and washing could wait. I put on some nice smoothing music and got on my computer. I wrote God a letter, something that I do regularly. I told him in detail exactly how I was feeling. The Scripture, "And let us not be weary in well doing; for in due season we shall reap if we faint not." Galatians 6:9 came to mind.

All of a sudden, I heard pots and pans clinging and water running in the sink! "Someone" is cleaning the kitchen, WOW!!

OK, my God, You are so Awesome!! Be not weary, be encouraged, Sister! God needs you to keep on praying, He hears you!! He will touch your husband's heart to lend a hand. You must set a standard of excellence and order in your home. You are the keeper of the house. Systems must be put into place and enforced. There should be designated household chores that are shared among all family members. It is your responsibility to convey your expectations. Some use calendars or send texts, just communicate. I have a separate laundry baskets for my husband and me. We both wash our clothes separately. I put the rubbish near the door; he takes it out when he leaves. We both load the dishwasher, I usually unload it. These actions are usually done without verbal request. I take charge of the maintenance of the house, vacuum, dusting, mopping etc. When my grandsons are in town, these automatically become their chores. It's simple and sweet. Get your house in order!

Let Us Pray

Father, Your command to get my house in order is loud and clear. I pray for Your wisdom, knowledge and understanding of how to maintain my house after the order is established. I thank You for enlisting my husband to assist me in these never- ending tasks. We thank You for our dwelling and we honor Your Presence there. I welcome You, Holy Spirit to our home; You have full reign. Thank You that my husband will help enforce and also abide by our established rules. Our rules are specific and our households flow without stress. Thank You that Your kingdom will come and Your will be done in our home, as well as, in heaven. In Jesus' Name, Amen!

Our Confession

Our home is heaven on earth! We have a Heavenly Marriage. God's kingdom has come and His will is being done in our home daily. I speak order into the universe, and may The Almighty be glorified in the heaven and on earth.

I Am Heavenly Married; Yes, I Am!!

Download 13:
You Are Never Alone!

It's a New Day, keep moving forward.

"A three-strand cord is not easily broken."
Ecclesiastes 4:12

Just a side note, don't let down your guard! Be mindful, that you ought to be consistently in prayer even during the holiday seasons, weekends and while on vacations. These are the times that our routines are altered. Be wise and pray. No time off, if you slack one day, you will lose territory.

This is a vision that I had one morning: I visualized a huge rock in the ocean. My goal was to reach that rock; my blessings were on that rock. I tossed a rope around the rock from my location. My goal was to hold on to the rope and start my journey, I remembered that the rock was my focus. I had to leave my comfort zone, the familiar, to get to the rock. I imagined all kinds of distractions and elements in the ocean between where I was and my destination.

Allow me to interpret the vision: The Rock is Your Anchor, God. You are focused, determined, and prayerful as you pace yourself. You are making progress every day.

Each day your connection to your source is vital. Often, your husband can be so busy that he doesn't connect; therefore, you must. *"Every good and perfect gift comes from God, the Father of Lights."* James 1:7. Seriously, your family's victories are dependent on your holding onto God. I pray that this vision will give you revelations of how much your husband needs you to hold on, not to them, but to GOD, the Father.

Let Us Pray

Father, I got it…You are our source. Thank You for providing for us. I repent for depending on my husband and not on You. I pray for my husband that as You are presently ministering to me, that he will experience a sign of relief. Help us both to focus on You when we begin our day. It would be so wonderful if we could come before Your presence together each morning! I am sure that would make You so happy. As I continue to hold on for our family's sake, I pray that Your son gets this revelation. Thank You for the vision, I really got it! Wow, in Jesus' Name. Amen!

Our Confession

Jesus is my rock and my anchor. I am focused on the prize of the high calling of Christ Jesus. I long for the day that I stand before Him and hear Him say "Well done, my good and faithful servant!"

I Am Heavenly Married; Yes, I Am!!

Download 14: Dynamite Prayer!!!

Not on my watch.

*"Be sober, be vigilant; because your adversary the devil,
as a roaring lion, walks about, seeking whom he may devour."*
1 Peter 5:8

Here is one of my favorite prayers:
"Lord, I ask that You sanctify all of my husband's
relationships, past and present. Amen"

Sanctify is defined as to make holy, consecrate, make free
from sin; purify, to make productive.

This is an ongoing prayer. As your husband meets new
people, move to new jobs, etc., you must cover him in
prayer.

The scriptures tell us to watch and pray. Always be
watchful and listen to your husband. There are times when

my husband is excited about a new associate, I take note of their name(s) and begin to pray for that person or group.

This Prayer of Relational Sanctification is also excellent for your children and yourself. Whenever, I meet someone, during our first prayer, I ask God to sanctify the relationship that we will be a blessing to one another and never bring any reproach to Him or each other." If the relationship is not good; it is usually short-lived.

This is a prayer, which I have lived by since 1980. It may take a while for it to become a habit; but I guarantee after several mishaps, you will commit to this prayer. I once heard someone say that people come into your life to add, subtract, multiply or divide. I watch over the affairs of my household, therefore, whenever someone new comes into our lives, I automatically pray this prayer of consecration. The devil is very subtle, he will try whatever and whomever to get into your marriage, children and home. The enemy is defeated because you are sober, watchful and praying!

Let Us Pray

Father, I ask that You would sanctify all of my husband's relationships; those of the past, present and future. Please remove those present relationships that are harmful to him. Open his eyes to recognize those people and environments that he should distance from. Make him a good judgment of people, with the strength to quickly bring a bad relationship to a halt. Thank You for bringing people into our lives to be a blessing to us. Allow us to be a blessing to them as well. Thank You, Jesus for praying for us, Amen!

Our Confession

I watch over the affairs of our household. I have 20/20 vision in the spirit. All of our relationships are sanctified. We are the head and not the tail. No weapon formed against us will prosper. I will speak Your blessings upon our family daily!

I Am Heavenly Married; Yes, I Am!!

Nugget: Queen, how are you looking today? Regardless of how you feel and what you are dealing with, your appearance and the fragrance of your attitude is key to victory!

Download 15:
The Heavy Artillery! Fasting

The difference between
Super and average.

*"Is this not the fast that I have chosen: to loosen the bonds
of wickedness, to undo the heavy burdens, to let the
oppressed go free, and that you break every yoke?"*
Isaiah 58.6

I hope that by now peace and harmony are norms at your
home. You are enjoying all your favorite foods and not
gaining a pound. I know, strange that I would mention
food. Well, when we are happy and things are going well,
we have a tendency to indulge our appetites, which is
usually my case.

This brings us to our next discipline, Dear Wife, *you need
to fast along with your praying.* Perhaps, you already have
this discipline intact and are regularly fasting. But, if not,
and you want to see serious change in yourself, *your*

husband and those that you are praying for, turn over your plate.

Please, pick up your bible and read Mark 9:14-29. You will find a family situation that was totally out of control. You know that if one member of the family is being tormented by the enemy, it will affect the entire family. Such was the case of this young boy that was set free from demons as a result of fasting and prayer! Jesus said, *"This kind cannot be driven out except by prayer and fasting."*

Reality Check: It is time for The Big Guns if you have been praying consistently and haven't seen major change, your husband needs you to F-A-S-T!!

Queen, it's true you are wonderful, but some situations will *never* change; unless someone gets serious enough to fast and pray, NO Exceptions! This is your answer; you have been praying about some things for a long time, but you haven't fasted. My question to you is, *are you willing to sacrifice to get the victory?*

The average person who is settling for an average life will rarely or never fast. So again, how bad do you want to live the supernatural life that God has planned for you? Think about it, if Jesus had to fast, it is a no brainer, you *need to fast.* You will know when and how. You will feel that nudge in your spirit or He may just speak to you. Most times, you will need a confirmation because you are trying hard not to understand this directive. Jesus gets it and will send the confirmation. Now, what are you going to do? You must heed to His instruction and fast. God doesn't lead us into a fast without a reason. I have found that when I'm instructed to fast, especially a lengthy fast, there's something life altering or threatening pending. I may be embarking on a new adventure, or the fast may save someone's life. Fasting along with prayer is a spiritual weapon that will defeat the devil every time. You can experience levels of victory that you will never realize without this discipline. How bad do you want it and are you willing to pay the price?

S.O.S...911...This is serious! Families for generations have been cursed because no one knew this or was unwilling to make the sacrifice.

Let Us Pray

Father, thank You for anointing my mind and imparting in me the discipline of fasting. Thank You, Jesus for sacrificing so that our family can receive the abundant life. I pray for bands of wickedness, heavy burdens, oppression and yokes to be destroyed in my husband and our family's lives. Please, teach us how to walk in the newness of life. Cause his life not to be the same, he is a new creature and is on fire for You! I thank You that he no longer settles for a second-class life. Open his eyes to see, as You see the world. Give him the discernment that is required to successfully navigate through this life. Expose every door that the enemy has gained access into his life and close it once and for all. He is the head and not the tail in every situation because You are present in his life. Cause him to be humble and realize that it is not by his power or might but it is through Your spirit that he moves and exists. In Jesus' Name, Amen!

Our Confession

I stand in the gap by consistently fasting and praying for nations, tribes and people of every tongue. I have been called to live a consecrated life. I declare that each time I fast according to Isaiah 58; bands of wickedness are loosened, yokes are broken, burdens lifted and the oppressed are set free!

I Am Heavenly Married; Yes, I Am!!

Bonus
"How, Why & Results of Fasting" Video
www.youtube.com: Bettie Rusher
https://youtu.be/A6cJ7s0bo2I

Download 16:
He Craves Your Respect!

Treat him like a man not a boy.

"...and calls those things which be not
as though they were."
Romans 4:7

Speak to the royalty in your husband! Your husband's primary need is for you to respect and honor him. I hesitate to use the word "submit" but we can't get around it. However, it is not such a bad thing once you understand that it is for your good. In 1 Peter 3 (read the entire chapter, good information), Sarah; Abraham's wife called him "lord" not Lord, notice the small l. I do that from time to time and my husband can't stop grinning. Imagine if you honor him every day as your lord how much difference this would make in your home. You may not be in agreement with what I am saying, so just pray about it. I realize that it is hard, especially when they are acting like a fool.

However, the wisdom in the matter is to speak to him as if he was walking in his lordship.

Meditate on that, Sis. I had to admit that I am challenged to really watch how I speak to all the men that are in my life; mainly my husband. I prayed and asked the Holy Spirit to help me to discern when I am speaking to the boy or fool instead of the man and king in them.

Let's assume that it is true that men have both a lord and fool inside. The manner in which you talk to God should be the same manner that you talk to your husband. Ok, take a deep breath…that's heavy. If that is the gauge, I, too, have missed it so many times. A king deserves respect, honor, and praise. Your thoughts regarding your husband should be kingly. The enemy will always put negative and foolish thoughts in your mind regarding your husband. These negative thoughts become words and we find ourselves talking to the fool in our husband. He then responds in the same manner.

Strive to master the art of talking to the lord in your husband. Begin to have kingdom conversations about matters of importance. A fool in a man majors in pettiness and the low life. Your new awareness will alter your outlook and conversations with your husband.

Let Us Pray

I humbly ask for Your forgiveness for the disrespectful manner in which I have talked to my husband. I can see that this goes back to my relationship with my father and even You, my Heavenly Father. I pray that he will respond to my change by allowing the king to arise. Allow the foolishness to die, in the Name of Jesus as it is no longer being nourished by my words. I thank You for the king that You have given me. Jesus, I see him as You see him, Amen!

Our Confession

My husband is a king. I am skillful in how I communicate with the king that is inside of him. He honors me as his good thing and receives Your favor every day!

I Am Heavenly Married; Yes, I Am!!

"He who finds a wife finds a good thing, and obtains favor from the LORD."
Proverbs 18.22

Download 17: Learn A Lesson From An Ex-Wife!

A lifetime lesson learned the hard way.

"She does him good and not evil
all the days of her life."
Proverbs 31.12

Dear Mrs. Bettie,

I don't understand, things are not working out as I planned. It has been seven years since I divorced him, time seems to fly. My ex-husband has remarried and seems to be happy. I don't understand, he treats her like a queen! I can't believe his vision that I honestly didn't support, finally came to pass. He really did work his plan to finish school and go into business. I don't understand why he didn't do all that while we were together. OK, I heard Mrs. New Wife is a praying woman and will cut you if you speak anything negative about him. I allowed so many factors to come between us; the children, our family, even my church responsibilities. If I hadn't listened to my unmarried girlfriends and not desired to hang out with them, things might have worked out. I could have prayed more and our family could be together. Honestly, I still love him but it's too late. Is it wrong to pray that they break up? I know...that's wrong. Jesus, forgive me and bless him and his new family. In the Most High's Name, Amen.

Please, pray for me.
Ms. I Am So Sad

Reality Check: He can be here today and gone tomorrow! Someone is at this very moment waiting and visualizing being his wife. What you don't want; another woman will gladly accept, polish up with some unconditional love and voila, a New Man!!

Let Us Pray

Father, I so appreciate being married to Your son. Forgive me for the thoughts I have when I am upset with him. Help me to pray for him even when I am angry. I know that I can't go back and the grass isn't greener on the other side. There is nothing out there for me but trouble. Help me to talk to the right people when I don't know what to do. I need patience, I know that You are working it out. But he can really get on my nerves. Bless and keep my husband. You know I do love him and never want to lose him. Help me, Jesus, Amen!

Our Confession

I am content. I will not complain. I honor my husband and realize that he is a jewel. I see the greatness in him in spite of his faults. I love my husband. No weapon formed against us shall prosper. Our marriage will stand the test of time!

I Am Heavenly Married; Yes, I Am!!

Download 18: A Heavenly Marriage!

You will see the fruit sooner or later.

"Violence shall no more be heard in thy land, wasting nor destruction within thy borders; but thou shalt call thy walls Salvation, and thy gates Praise."
Isaiah 60:18

One Saturday morning, *my* husband said something that had me smiling the rest of the day! You want to know what it was, right?

I shared earlier how I had prayed for Peace and Harmony in our marriage. Well, last week whenever our conversations would get a little heated, I would claim Peace and Harmony out loud in his hearing. It is amazing, how we both would instantly shut up.

Well, this particular morning, I was *speaking my mind*; when he had the nerve to say, *"Peace and Harmony."* I shut my mouth and smiled the rest of the day. My Lady, it works!

Your words are creating an atmosphere everywhere you go. Peace and Harmony are contagious, and once you have it you literally can't live without it. Be encouraged today to continue on this journey. You may not see immediate results; it may appear to be getting worse. Persevere, you will see your fruit if you continue and don't give up. Most times, the work is being done on the inside of us, so watch out when your husband starts to preach and correct you with the same words. Prepare yourself to be able to handle the change. It is coming!

Let Us Pray

Father, by faith my husband is changing even if I don't see it. Please, continue the work that You have begun in both of us. I believe that as I am praying each and every day, that You hear and answers me. You have a perfect plan for Your son and I thank You that I am instrumental to his destiny. I pray that You would continue to draw us to You. Remove the obstacles that prevent us from running to You. Deliver us from all lust, egotism, and pride. Wash us Oh God with the marvelous blood of Jesus until we are white as snow, Amen!

Our Confession

I see the change in my husband and it is marvelous in my sight. I am prepared to embrace the new man that God has created. I am his helpmate. I will continue to speak positive words over him. He is made in your image! Prayer is powerful, as I pray for him, I am getting better too. Yea!

I Am Heavenly Married; Yes, I Am!!

Just Checking!!
Has praying for your husband
become a daily habit?

Download 19: Hold On, Your Help Is Here!!!

Mama said there would be days like this.

"He gives power to the faint; and to him who has no might, He increases strength."
Isaiah 40:29

Queen, I know you never felt like this...but, one day I was at the end of the road, I wanted out of this marriage. I was just tired and didn't have the strength to work on it, nor the desire to even pray about it. I was done! I thought that there was nothing more that I could do.

That was my attitude as I deposited my tired body into the pew at church one Sunday morning.

The Speaker began with a question, *"How many of you are at the end of the road in your marriages, jobs, school...?"*

He proceeded to describe my then/present situation. I didn't want to hear the rest of the message because I knew I was going to get just what I needed. Which was to simply *ask God for more Grace,* God's ability that is always available to us. I always thought that Grace was God's unmerited favor, but there's more that He desires to give us. Truly, I *was* exhausted, I just needed to receive more Power to keep on going until the task was accomplished or the desire was obtained. Well, that was my answer but I didn't want an answer, I wanted out!

Some of you are at that point today, and God just gave you your answer. Sister, humble yourselves as I did and *ask for more Grace*; His ability and power to accomplish His Will in your life.

That was in 2005, I must admit that I have asked for more Grace many times since. God is faithful, He knows how much we can bear, and will equip us to go through whatever He allows us to confront. I am so happy that I didn't stay at home that day and missed that message, it has made a difference in my life. I wouldn't be able to share this with you, right? It was truly a word in season to this weary soul.

Let Us Pray

Father, thank You for Your overcoming strength. I pray for my husband, Your son. You know the days when he is at the point of quitting. Sometimes, I can see the stress in his eyes and the weariness of his body. I pray for more Grace in both of our lives. I desire to be understanding and be there to help him. Yet, move me out of the way when he should be relying on You. Thank You for being all things to us. We love you, Jesus, Amen!

Our Confession

God's Grace is sufficient for me. When I am weak, His Grace strengthens me. I have the power to continue to the finish line; I will not faint. We win!

I Am Heavenly Married; Yes, I Am!!

Bonus Video
"Message to Wives, Hold On"
https://youtu.be/5EUbUHrNDLY
www.youtube.com: Bettie Rusher

Download 20:
See What You See!

You are the queen of his castle.

*"She watches over the ways of her household,
and does not eat the bread of idleness."*
Proverbs 31.27

Sister, take the time to walk through every room of your home to *see what you see*. When was the last time you surveyed your child's room, including their closets? Is your teenager's room off limits? How about your husband's office? This is a routine that should be done periodically throughout the year. Purge old mail and magazines. I had to discontinue unrequested ungodly magazines that had randomly started to come to our home.

In our busyness, we overlook stuff, and ungodly things can creep into our homes. Proverbs 31.27 says the Virtuous Woman kept watch (spied, observed closely) over her household. She surveyed to see what she would see.

Sometimes discoveries are made that need your immediate attention. Ignoring situations won't make them disappear. It truly takes boldness and strength to deal head on with an uncomfortable issue. As you continue to pray for your husband and family, the light will expose the darkness. It is better to embrace the truth and deal with the situation.

As you go through each corner of your home, call out the Name of Jesus. I challenge you to sanctify the entire house this week with the His Name.

Let Us Pray

Father, I pray that You would sanctify our home. Holy Spirit, lead me as I survey our home; expose any darkness that may have entered our dwelling. I pray that my husband would not be drawn to any ungodly devices. Sanctify the atmosphere of any pornography, witchcraft or the like. I thank You for my sensitivity to recognize when evil has entered our home. Thank You, Jesus for a spirit of cleanliness and order in every corner of our home, Amen!

Our Confession

I watch and pray every day. Nothing gets past me because of the Holy One that resides in me. My house is naturally and spiritually clean and in order. No form of darkness can dwell in our home!

I Am Heavenly Married; Yes, I Am!!

Download 21:
Stir Up Some Excitement!

It's time to take it up a notch.

"...where the Spirit of the Lord is,
there is liberty."
2 Corinthians 3:17

Today, I felt so good that I got busy creating new energy in our master suite. I felt like playing house, that's when I began to move furniture around like I did as a little girl playing in my make-believe home. I re-arranged the sofa, chair and ottoman. I added some of our recent personal photos (I have only pictures of us in our private space). I borrowed a plant, lamp, and picture from another room.

I finished just as he walked in and with a look of surprise, turned around, and said, *"I can live with this!"*

Your husband needs this movement in every area. Boredom can set in quickly. The need for something different is often the reason men stray. The bedroom is that sacred place for your husband to unwind and bare his nakedness. Yes, your bedroom should be sexy; does it draw your husband? Does your bed have that luxury hotel feel; if not, why not? An investment in good pillows and coverings may just be what the doctor ordered. A live plant in your bedroom brings life as you watch its growth and beauty. Music, scents, and wall color make a room cozy. Perhaps a few wall pictures or photo of you and hubby on vacation will add spice. You must think outside the box and allow fresh ideas to enter your mind.

Queen, you have to keep it *fresh* by creating *movements*. Where there is no movement, things can get stale. Total cost for the new look, not one cent. I am good in here for a few months.

Let Us Pray

Father, I thank You for showing me how to please my husband. I pray that my husband's heart is right here at home. Help me to create an atmosphere that draws him home each day. Cause him to love to entertain his family and friends at home. During his home time, allow him to dream and visualize Your plans. Holy Spirit, I invite You into our bedchambers. Enhance our sacred place with Your presence. In Jesus' Mighty Name I pray, Amen.

Our Confession

I'm sugar and spice and everything nice. I please my husband so much that he runs home every day. I am hospitable and always prepared to entertain his friends and family. Our home is sexy and pleasing to all five senses. God's presence is in every nook and cranny. Our home is a place of refuge!

I Am Heavenly Married; Yes, I Am!!

Download 22:
Serenade Your Man!

If you don't *know* how, *learn* the skill.

**"Marriage is honorable and
the bed is undefiled."
Hebrews 13.4**

Let's get some serenading tips from the book of Song of Solomon 5:10 CEV. The skillful wife declares that her man is "handsome and healthy, the most outstanding among ten thousand."

She proceeds to serenade her man:
"Awake, O North wind,
And come, O South wind
Blow upon my garden,
That its spices may flow out.
Let my beloved come to his garden
And eat its pleasant fruits."

Her man cheerfully responds:
"I have come to my garden,
My sister, my spouse;
I have gathered my myrrh with my spice;
I have eaten my honeycomb with my honey
I have drunk my wine with my milk."
Ladies, this is in your bible.
Song of Solomon 4:16-5:1 KJV

Early one morning after praying for my handsome and healthy husband (I'm a quick learner), I was reading these verses and got a revelation. I am not going to tell you my interpretation; but what do you think she really mean by "garden". Also, how many times is "my" mentioned in his response?

I absolutely love the bible; it covers every subject that pertains to life and godliness. Here it plainly talks about sex and romance. Which we know is very different, you can have sex without romance. What do you do when that is the case? You don't just ignore your desire and accept the unfulfillment. First of all, prayer does change things. Talking with your husband about the lack of romance and/or other intimate issues is important. He may not be aware of the fact that you are dissatisfied. You must remember to be very selective of the words that you use; this is a delicate subject. Also, pray about what you can do differently to bring about the closeness you desire. Read the Song of Solomon together at least once a month, it really can't hurt. Begin to use the dialogue that the wife used to express her love and emotions. Rap on my sister, have fun!

Check Up: This may just be what the doctor ordered. You may need to relax and loosen up! Turn down the lights and serenade your husband. Skillfully, encourage him to play in "his" garden.

Let Us Pray

Father, I thank you for Your Word. You didn't leave out anything. I appreciate the joy of sex and having an intimate relationship with my husband. Help him to drop down all walls of inhibition with me. He deserves a virtuous woman that he can safely trust, make me that woman. Erase all of the past experiences from his mind. Remove thoughts of other women and places that interfere with our intimacy. I appreciate the Blood of Jesus that washes our minds, body and soul. During the moments of sharing our bodies, keep our minds from wandering to other people and places. Keep our minds and hearts right there to fully connect with one another and You. Our marriage bed is undefiled. In Jesus' Name, Amen!

Our Confession

I am skillful at serenading my husband. He has eyes for me only! The atmosphere in our boudoir is getting sweeter and sweeter every night!

I Am Heavenly Married; Yes, I Am!!

Download 23: What Fragrance Are You Wearing?

My private blend, one of a kind.

"It is better to live alone in the
corner of an attic,
than with a quarrelsome wife
in a lovely home."
Proverbs 21:9

Or better yet; "It's better to live
alone in the desert
than with a quarrelsome, complaining wife."
Proverbs 21.19

OK, one more; "A quarrelsome wife
is as annoying
as constant dripping on a rainy day."
Proverbs 27:15

OUCH!! If the shoe fits, wear it. Queen, now tell the truth... are you a Complainer, a Chronic Nagger? Yes or No? Be honest with yourself, everyone knows. You may do it without thinking, it may be a trait that runs in your family; of never being satisfied.

Sisters, don't chase your husband away.

This is straight and to the point; does your husband have one foot out the door? If so, thank God for this lesson. Your Unconditional Love can pull him back to you.

Your first step toward freedom is to admit it, then ask God for forgiveness and the strength to change. You also need to confess this fault to your husband and ask his forgiveness for torturing him. It's really that simple, you are free, My Sister!

You are now free to pray and command peace and harmony into your home; and kindness to your husband, now friend. Practice being sweet. Wow, that sounds so simple but kindness has to be cultivated. It is one of the fruit of the spirit, it is in you but needs to be stirred up. It was easy to complain but now you will need to consciously slow down to think and not speak negative words. It is truly a new set of skills that you can master. Your husband needs you to be sweet. One day, my husband actually prayed out loud, "Lord, make my wife sweeter." His request shocked me; I didn't realize that I wasn't sweet. I had become an expert complainer; I could list his faults 1 to 100 within ten minutes. If asked to list his good qualities, I honestly couldn't without straining to list ten. How sad! I only focused on the negative and overlooked all the wonderful traits that he possesses. I'm so glad that God isn't that way.

Let Us Pray

Forgive me for being a nagger and a complainer. I desire to be sweet and kind to my husband. Please, repair the damage that has been done to him. Allow my sweet words to heal any pain or negative thoughts that he may have towards me. Thank You for keeping him from sweet and enticing words of other women. Strengthen my husband in the areas that you know that he is weak. I will begin today to celebrate his strengths and pray about his weaknesses. Give my husband the courage to change and not run from your correction. I will not be the excuse for him to run away. I thank you for the mighty work that you are doing under the roof of this home. In Jesus' Name, Amen!

Our Confession

I'll forever praise my husband. I look beyond his faults and honor his strengths. The law of kindness is in my mouth. Our marriage is exciting and full of adventure, and an example to the world. It feels good to wear God's sweetness!

I Am Heavenly Married; Yes, I Am!!

Download 24:
The Power of God's Smile!

Smile, it's candid camera.

"Whatever you sow, you shall reap."
Galatians 6:7

God truly has a sense of humor! I hope you are participating in the challenge to make your husband smile. I am having fun with this. He doesn't know how to handle the extra attention. I pray that you are having fun, too, while learning something new about your man. I enjoy seeing my husband smile so much, I am going to make this a habit.

However, this is the joke! I smile more than he does. It is nearly impossible to create a smile and not smile yourself. I'm walking with a permanent smile, truly this is funny. God's smile will open closed doors!

Keep smiling, beautiful lady!

Let Us Pray

Father, You are so funny! Yes, we are smiling more these days. A little extra effort goes a long way. I pray for Your son that he freely receives my gestures of love. Remove any walls of insecurity and inhibitions to receive Your love. I realize that the smile begins within. I pray that all throughout the day, Your son's intentions are to return home, to his place of refuge. Always, remind me that I have the power to make him smile. Jesus, continue to do an inside job on us both. Smiles to You, Amen!

Our Confession

I can feel my Father's smile and it's beautiful. I will commit to smile throughout this day; regardless to the circumstances. My smile will bring deliverance to others. They will see God through my eyes as I smile. I want to be used by Him today!

I Am Heavenly Married; Yes, I Am!!

Just Checking!!
Did you make your bed today?
Strange question?
It really makes a difference to your husband.
Most men love a clean and orderly environment.

Download 25:
There is a Flow!

Being at the right place, right time with the right attitude.

"But Martha was distracted with much serving, and she approached Him and said, "Lord, do You not care that my sister has left me to serve alone? Therefore, tell her to help me." And Jesus answered and said to her, "Martha, Martha, you are worried and troubled about many things. But one thing is needed, and Mary has chosen that good part, which will not be taken away from her."
Luke 10:40-42

Queen, just slow down and take a seat! Sometimes, you need to remind yourself to slow down, breathe, and pace yourself. This world's system is on fast forward; its design is to never allow you to slow down. You find yourself speeding, trying to keep up; or, being busy doing one thing while your mind is on something else. Slow down, breathe, and connect with Your God. He is speaking to you right now, cautioning you, showing you a better way. Oftentimes, mistakes are made because you are moving too fast. Slow down, My Sister.

Did you slow down long enough to pray for your husband? Is he on the fast track, too? Someone has to slow down or disaster is around the corner. You can't keep this pace; you are the one person that can s-l-o-w it down. You really don't want God to force you to slow down. He has a way to put on the brakes.

One morning, I woke up with severe pain in my back. I couldn't move without pain. I had to literally stay in bed for a couple of days. It was very difficult having to wait for someone to assist in every way. During that time; I was forced to slow down to think about my life. Ever since that day, I truly count it a blessing to be up and about my Father's Business as I control my life's rhythm.

Our husbands can also be guilty of this. I have placed a plaque near my husband's desk that says, "Slow me down, Lord." I am sure that from time to time, he notices it.

Personally, I noticed that I make mistakes when I'm moving too fast. Why is it that we have the time to redo a task when we could have done it right the first time? Most errors cost us money. Therefore, it behooves us to learn how to flow with the Holy Spirit and move at His pace. We don't want to get ahead of God.

Let Us Pray

Father, thank You for wisdom to slow down and live in the moment. Help my husband to take the time to sit down to eat and actually enjoy the meal; literally, taking time to smell the coffee. Deliver him from the rat race of the society. Show my husband what adjustments he must make to align his life with You. Thank You for the designated time for the family and me. I believe our slowing down is going to make a difference in every area of our lives. Keep working with us, Jesus, Amen!

Our Confession

I live a balanced life. I pace myself and allow the Holy Spirit to lead me. I live life one moment at a time. My husband watches me as I flow with God and mimics my ways. I will bring my husband good and not harm all the days of my life!

I Am Heavenly Married; Yes, I Am!!

Download 26:
Watch, as Well as, Listen!

Having eyes and ears to hear his heart.

"Two are better than one because they have a good reward for their labor. For if they fall, one will lift up his companion. But woe to him who is alone when he falls, for he has no one to help him up."
Ecclesiastes 4:9 and 10

"Aw, Man!" was my husband's cry one morning as we were driving into work. He had forgotten an important item that he needed to finish a project. He realized that he had driven too far to turn around. He thought, *I have to come up with another plan.*

I was quietly riding beside him, engulfed in reading my bible and was alarmed by his outcry. He had such a disappointed look on his face. My heart really went out to him, especially because I noticed that he had been under a lot of pressure that week. He had been forgetting things, was short-tempered and exhausted. I began to pray that God would fix things for him that day. As I prayed God's love and compassion flooded my heart. Even though, he still had this "I don't know what to do look", I knew God had heard me.

Queen, as a wise wife, you must *watch* and *listen* to *your* husband and pray accordingly. Check out his body language, what is he not saying verbally? Often, asking questions only makes the situation worse. God will lead you as you continue to pray daily for your husband. Discern, when God is dealing with him and he is taking his frustrations out on you. Pray about it and keep your mind on God, don't try to figure out his complexity, you will end up with a headache.

Listening is a lost art, ask God for it. This learned skill can make you very valuable to your husband and to God's family. People need someone that care enough to genuinely listen.

Let Us Pray

Father, anoint me to be an excellent helpmate for Your son. I come into agreement with Jesus' prayers for my husband. Thank you, Jesus, for making intercessions for us all. As Your son goes about this day, I pray that he recognizes and acknowledges Your presence. I pray that he has all that he requires to have a perfect day. Teach him to call on You in his time of distress. I thank You for drawing him closer and closer. Deal with my husband, Holy Spirit. In Jesus' Name, Amen!

Our Confession

Every day, I watch and listen to my husband. I can see a great change in him. I like what I see. He is the man of my dreams. Only God could have done this wonderful thing, right before my eyes. I serve an Awesome God!

I Am Heavenly Married; Yes, I Am!!

Download 27:
In Sickness and in Health!

A Woman of Integrity, Keeps Her Word.

Yes, you said it. When you uttered those vows, more thought and emphasis were on "the health" part of the vow. We always want to see our husbands being strong and vigorous, but there may be days when they are not as strong.

After 30 plus years of marriage; our bodies have changed quite a bit. We are both in good health, but it requires maintenance. We eat differently, very seldom spurge on pizza and soda. We exercise often and strive to drink more water. We help each other to stay on the course.

Why, did we change? Our bodies told us that we had to. Therefore, why wait until your body starts to decline before you begin to take care of yourself? It is a good idea to begin now. If you are knowingly abusing your body; how long do you think it will be before it reacts?

Really notice your husband. Don't nag if he still smokes, drinks alcohol, and/or eat unhealthy foods. Just pray for him and you start making healthy choices. He will see the new you and most times follow your example, especially when the Holy Spirit nudges him.

I had gone out of town one weekend; I was exhausted and wanted to take a shower and go directly to bed. My husband was waiting on my return to take him to the hospital…long story short…it was a life-threatening wake up call. He was in the hospital for a couple of days, which gave him an opportunity to slow down to assess his lifestyle. He made the decision to live longer and do whatever it takes to take our grandchildren on a cruise that he had planned. God has a way of changing your husband without you saying a word, prayer changes things.

This is a serious subject, think about it…your health is so important. You want to be around to see the glory on your husband. God is going to answer your prayers, you want to be around to enjoy the fruit of your labor.

Just for the record; we did take our grandchildren on a cruise and spent two heart-binding weeks with them at our home. We will cherish the memories forever. Life is so sweet, every moment to be savored.

Let Us Pray

Father, thank you for one more day in the land of the living. Help me to appreciate every moment that I share with my husband, not knowing if it is our last one together. Thank You for his overall health. Show me what I can do to enhance his life in every area. Show him the areas that he needs to make adjustments in his lifestyles. Crystalize the vision that you have for him. Give him a sign, show him a glimpse of what you have planned and prepared for him. Give your son that power to press towards that mark of excellency. In Jesus' Name, Amen!

Our Confession

I declare that we are healthy, wealthy, wise and happy!

I Am Heavenly Married; Yes, I Am!!

Side Note: I'm committed to providing a healthy breakfast every morning for my husband. Knowing that he will consume fast food or not eat at all as he rushes about his workday. It gives me comfort knowing that he starts his day with the most important meal cooked by yours truly.

Download 28: Laugh at the Devil Truly a Weapon!

Become skillful at doing the unexpected.

"...the joy of the Lord is your strength."
Nehemiah 8:10

Imagine this! You and husband are returning home from a romantic resort vacation. You are driving along Lakeshore Drive, sunroof opened, his favorite music is playing and the breeze is gently caressing your hair. What a perfect summer day, with the sun reflecting on the lake as the seagulls played.

What is wrong with this picture? Both you and hubby are upset and wearing a frown. What happened? One wrong word changed everything! You don't know what to say to fix this. You realized that the enemy has created this mess.

You both are shocked, neither wanting to say anything to make it worse, so you are silently riding along on this beautiful route, that may be a once in a lifetime moment, dumbfounded.

Yes, that happened to us! It is amazing how things can be so beautiful and in a moment a storm hits. Of course, I prayed for wisdom, the devil had to go! I had a thought; *start to laugh out loud.* After thinking, how stupid is that; I busted out with a fake laugh. You can imagine the look on my husband's face; he thought I had lost my mind. His shocked expression made me "really" laugh. Soon, he began to laugh at me. The atmosphere instantly changed and we both were joyfully belly laughing; peace and harmony had been restored, the devil was once again defeated.

Laughing out loud has extinguished many awkward moments in our walk together. It is very difficult, almost impossible to hold on to a grudge or attitude when your mate can laugh at the situation. My husband has really become skillful at using this method to change my negative behavior.

Sister, pray that your husband will laugh more.

"A cheerful heart is good medicine,
but a broken spirit saps a person's strength."
Proverbs 17.22 NLT

Let Us Pray

Father, help me to always remember this strategy when I don't know what to do or say. I thank You for the power to change the atmosphere. I get the revelation; the devil hates to see us laugh. Please, reinforce this lesson not to take life so seriously. I thank You that Your son is responsive. Program us to love to laugh and to enjoy the Abundant Life that You have given us. I pray in Jesus' Almighty Name, Amen!

Our Confession

The sacrifice of Jesus was not in vain. I received my salvation and deliverance. I live the Abundant Life that He died to give us. Laughter is something I do on a daily basis. My laughter is music to my husband and the Father's ears.

I Am Heavenly Married; Yes, I Am!!

Download 29:
What's Your Sabbath Time?

Only the wise woman will practice this regimen.

"Come ye yourselves apart into
a desert place,
and rest a while..."
Mark 6: 31

Sabbath Monday! I always look forward to Mondays because as you know, it is my sabbath day. I love having a relaxed day of not pressing to do anything. I slow down to water my plants and to actually talk to them. I bet that they are rejoicing as I love on them. I usually leisurely wash and fold a few loads of laundry, it's good to start the week off with an empty laundry hamper.

Yes, we are at the end of this volume and I'm mentioning it again. It is for your good to select your day or sabbath time? Remember, once you determine your sabbath, you must announce your declaration to your world. To start, you may not be able to take an entire day but designate an evening to shut the door to the world.

This would be a wonderful time to spend some quality time praying for your hubby. Quality doesn't necessarily mean all day but undistracted, focused prayer on your man's behalf. How about scheduling a picnic with Jesus? Or imagine, a bubble bath, good music and a book in the middle of the day, it's your time, enjoy!!

Queen, you have learned how to seriously and systemically defeat the enemy on every hand. These spiritual weapons are simple yet powerful; you just have to incorporate them into your daily life. Remember, David killed the giant, Goliath, with one smooth stone.

Let Us Pray

Father, thank You for this wonderful day to relax and recharge. I desire to unload all the baggage of disappointments, failure and any other toxic matter that I picked up last week. Help me to stay focused. I pray for my husband's spiritual life today. I believe that You are performing surgery on both of us. I pray that he would seek You more today than he did yesterday. Please, don't let my husband be lost. I know that it is not Your will that any man perishes but for all to receive eternal life. What can I do to help my husband pray and read Your Word more? Thank You for making me slow down and look in the mirror this sabbath day. In Jesus' Name, Amen!

Confession

I get it! My sabbath is the secret to my longevity. I have a delightful life because of the quality time I spend with the Father. My life is so enriched that the overflow blesses many. I'm blessed to be a blessing!

I Am Heavenly Married; Yes, I Am!!

Download 30: Ask and You Shall Receive!

Secret: Your husband loves to brag on you.

*"Her husband is respected at the city gates,
where he takes his seat among
the elders of the land."*
Proverbs 31:23

The Virtuous Wife's husband was sharp! I am sure that she had a lot to do with his exalted position.

The most important thing is; what are you speaking about your husband? Are you blessing him with your tongue every day?

Your husband hasn't nearly reached his potential! What you see is not all you get! Marriage is wonderful, it is ever-evolving. After many years of marriage, each of you will change so much. Marriage is a gift that keeps peeling back layers of love. Regardless of the stage or season of your marriage; look forward to better days. Remember, you create with your words? How awesome is your husband? Are you sticking with your proclamations of your husband's greatness? God is still creating, shaping and molding you and your him.

Imagine your husband doing and saying all the things that you desire. Now, begin to speak those things that you desire to see. It feels weird at first, but it works. Remember, it is what you do behind closed doors that matters to God. Here are the words that I speak about my husband: "My husband is a man that seeks God daily, he is drawn to God's Word. He is a man of strength, integrity, and walks in love. He is trustworthy and reliable. He loves his family and plans quality time to be with us. He loves to take trips to exotic places. He is a peacemaker. He is a man with a vision that he is working on every day. He doesn't sit in front of the television for hours and hours. My husband is aware of the times and helps others. He sits among the elders of the gates where he shares his wisdom and experience! The atmosphere in our home is getting sweeter and sweeter every day!"

Reality Check: Someone besides you wants *your* man. Sis, do the work!

Let Us Pray

Father, I thank You for my awesome husband. Thank You for the new light that I see upon Your son. You are so faithful to continue the work that You have begun in us. I look forward to the days ahead as we continue to be unveiled to ourselves and the world. You didn't make junk and are totally committed to making us. You have the power to bring the necessary changes in Your time. I appreciate every change, be it small or large. I see Your hand at work, he isn't the same man that I married. I see a beautiful masterpiece that You are skillfully molding for the world to see. Wow, in Jesus' Name I pray, Amen!

Our Confession

I do not miss a day praying for Your son. He is a polished gem and has grown to appreciate me. We are Your trophy, set upon a hill. I have faith to speak into manifestation Your greatness in our lives for the world to see. We are intentionally careful when complimented to give You all the Glory!

I Am Heavenly Married; Yes, I Am!!

Download 31:
Epilogue – I Must Practice What I Teach!

**Allow me to shine at the
end of the day.**

*"Be angry, and do not sin,
do not let the sun go down on your wrath."*
Ephesians 4:26

As I complete volume one of the Heavenly Marriage series, I find myself being tried and tested on everything that I have written. Imagine this, we are cruising along the Gulf of Mexico Ocean on a perfect day; we were on a Getaway in Cancun. (I purposely didn't call it a vacation because I was working on finishing this book.) We were merrily sailing along when he severely hurt my feelings. My emotions instantly went from peaceful to "you better praise God that we are in public mode." I was smoking on the inside. How could he allow this to happen? He quickly realized that he had a made a *big mistake* and quickly apologized verbally to God, and then to me. He was surprised that I didn't quickly change my disposition since he apologized. I really didn't want to accept his apology; well, not right away!

Every lesson that I have shared with you came to mind. I realized that this was a test and I had to pass with flying colors. My husband was trying so hard to get me to smile but I could not. I was really hurting inside and didn't want to smile. Yet, I really didn't want to ruin this perfect day. I really needed God's help to get past this, the devil had hit me with a surprised punch. So, I began to strategize…

I began to work on smiling within, then a self-imposed smile which was a ha-ha under my breath came. A laugh surfaced as I began to feel better because I was defeating this enemy. Instead of replaying what my husband did that upset me, I began to think about all the good qualities of my husband, including how cute he was looking. I then went to another area of the boat to pray. I began to dance and lift my hands praising God for such a beautiful day. 20 minutes later, he came to find me but didn't say a word, just sat quietly enjoying the scenery and music. When the boat pulled up at the dock; we both had a sigh of relief. He walked off ahead of me with a slight attitude.

Then God took over; we had met a beautiful couple that morning as we waited to board. They were going to the same island via another craft. When they saw us, they were wildly waving and grinning as they ran to approach us. I started a conversation with the wife, and the husbands proceeded to share their adventures. When we departed our ways, they never knew how they had helped us get over the *bridge over troubled waters*! Our evening was great; quiet dinner and early to bed, another Heavenly Married day in God's Kingdom!

Let Us Pray

Thank You, Father, for helping me to get through every test regardless of the intensity or length. Thank You, Holy Spirit for bringing back to my remembrance these lessons that I have downloaded. You told me in Your Word that we would have challenging days in our marriages. However, we can have victory even on those days. Let us never let the sun go down and we are angry with one another. Help us to be slow to anger and quick to get over it. I pray that Your son and our children learn these lessons by watching my behavior. As I walk out these simple yet powerful truths, allow me to be the angel to help another sister-wife in need! Love you, Father, Jesus, and Holy Spirit, Amen!

Our Confession

I accept the charge to share this wisdom with other wives. I am a wise woman that isn't controlled by my emotions. I am sensible and God-centered. When I feel myself being pulled into a place where flesh is in control, I have the resources to counteract. I am matured and quick to deal with offenses. I am an example to my husband; he beholds my chaste behavior with respect and is won to Christ without me preaching to him. I have a meek and quiet spirit and proud to be called one of Sarah's Daughters.

I Am Heavenly Married; Yes, I Am!!

Bonus
"My Go To Scriptures" E-Book download
These are some of the scriptures that help me
to do right when I want to do wrong!
www.backtoeden.today

It has been a pleasure and a challenge sharing our Heavenly Marriage with you. I hope that your marriage has been blessed by ours. Please, commit to practicing what you have received.

I look forward to hearing your testimonies as you continue your Heavenly Married Journey!

Peace and Harmony!
Mrs. Bettie J. Rusher

P.S. Please, leave a positive review @ www.amazon.com and go to www.backtoeden to sign up for the mailing list to stay informed of Bettie's upcoming books and webinars!

The Virtuous Wife

Proverbs 31:10-31 CEV

[10] A truly good wife
is the most precious treasure
a man can find!
[11] Her husband depends on her,
and she never
lets him down.
[12] She is good to him
every day of her life,
[13] and with her own hands
she gladly makes clothes.
[14] She is like a sailing ship
that brings food
from across the sea.
[15] She gets up before daylight
to prepare food
for her family
and for her servants.
[16] She knows how to buy land
and how to plant a vineyard,

[17] and she always works hard.
[18] She knows when to buy or sell,
and she stays busy
until late at night.
[19] She spins her own cloth,
[20] and she helps the poor
and the needy.
[21] Her family has warm clothing,
and so she doesn't worry
when it snows.
[22] She does her own sewing,
and everything she wears
is beautiful.
[23] Her husband is a well-known
and respected leader
in the city.
[24] She makes clothes to sell
to the shop owners.
[25] She is strong and graceful,
as well as cheerful
about the future.
[26] Her words are sensible,
and her advice
is thoughtful.
[27] She takes good care
of her family
and is never lazy.
[28] Her children praise her,
and with great pride
her husband says,

[29] "There are many good women,
but you are the best!"
[30] Charm can be deceiving,
and beauty fades away,
but a woman
who honors the LORD
deserves to be praised.
[31] Show her respect—
praise her in public
for what she has done.

Acknowledgements

Certainly, there would not be a book series had it not been for my husband, Kenneth Rusher. Words cannot adequately express my heart's sentiments, only GOD knows how going through life with a partner can weld two hearts together. Thank you, Kenny, for your unconditional love and patience; I realize that I too am a work in progress.

I must give honor to my only birth child, Venna, who has been there from the beginning. You have unconditionally loved us through it all. Thank you for always encouraging us in our marriage and not divorcing us.

The list continues; there have been so many that have walked with us during this journey, too many to mention. It truly takes a village to hold a marriage together. Thank you all for your love, we covet your continual prayers.

Hallelujah, it is finished!! Truly, I struggled as I wrote the words of this book, mostly because I felt so inadequate because of the high and lows of our marriage. I don't claim to be an expert in the Art of Marriage. However, through it all, we are a witness that, with GOD, all things are possible.

With Love, BettieR

Bonus Chapter:
My Go To Scriptures

Here is a list of 25 scriptures that I go to when I need a quick pick me up. These verses will bring you peace, strength, and wisdom in your lowest moments. It would be good to memorize them and quote them out loud. Hearing the Word is more effective than just reading the scriptures.

There have been seasons where I would fight the devil with two or three scriptures. I would memorize them and whenever necessary I would cut him deep with the Word of God. The Word is a sword and can be used both defensively and offensively. When negative thoughts would come into my mind; I combat by thinking or quoting out loud My Go To Scriptures. Satan respects the Word of God and will be shocked when you began to use this ammunition to defeat him. Shouting and cussing will not move him, only the Word of God.

Psalms 40:1-3

"I waited patiently for the LORD and He inclined to me, and heard my cry. He also brought me up out of a horrible pit, out of the miry clay, and set my feet upon a rock, and established my steps. He has put a new song in my mouth— Praise to our God, many will see it and fear and will trust in the LORD."

Psalms 126:5
"Those who sow in tears shall reap in joy."

Corinthians 10:13
"No temptation has overtaken you except such as is common to man; but God is faithful, who will not allow you to be tempted beyond what you are able, but with the temptation will also make the way of escape, that you may be able to bear it."

Isaiah 54:17
"No weapon formed against you shall prosper and every tongue which rises against you in judgment you shall condemn.

This is the heritage of the servants of the LORD and their righteousness is from Me, says the LORD."

Galatians 6:9
"And let us not grow weary while doing good, for in due season we shall reap if we do not lose heart."

2 Timothy 1:7

*The first verse that I memorized!

"For God has not given us the spirit of fear; but power, and of love, and a sound mind."

James 1:4

"But let patience have its perfect work, that you may be perfect and complete, lacking nothing."

James 1:5

"If any of you lacks wisdom, let him ask of God, who gives to all liberally and without reproach, and it will be given to him."

Ephesians 6:10-20

The Whole Armor of God

"[10] Finally, my brethren, be strong in the Lord and in the power of His might.

[11] Put on the whole armor of God that you may be able to stand against the wiles of the devil.

[12] For we do not wrestle against flesh and blood, but against principalities, against powers, against the rulers of the darkness of this age, against spiritual hosts of wickedness in the heavenly places.

[13] Therefore take up the whole armor of God that you may be able to withstand in the evil day, and having done all, to stand.

[14] Stand therefore, having girded your waist with truth, having put on the breastplate of righteousness,

[15] and having shod your feet with the preparation of the gospel of peace;

[16] above all, taking the shield of faith with which you will be able to quench all the fiery darts of the wicked one.

[17] And take the helmet of salvation, and the sword of the Spirit, which is the Word of God."

Deuteronomy 28:13

"And the LORD will make you the head and not the tail; you shall be above only, and not be beneath, if you heed the commandments of the LORD your God, which I command you today, and are careful to observe them."

Psalms 144:1

"Blessed be the LORD my Rock. Who trains my hands for war and my fingers for battle."

Hebrews 13:5

"Let your conduct be without covetousness; be content with such things as you have. For He Himself has said, "I will never leave you nor forsake you."

Psalms 91:11

"For He shall give His angels charge over you to keep you in all your ways."

Luke 18:1

"Then He spoke a parable to them, that men always ought to pray and not lose heart."

Ephesians 3:20

"Now to Him who is able to do exceedingly abundantly above all that we ask or think, according to the power that works in us."

Colossians 3:23-24

"And whatever you do, do it heartily, as to the Lord and not to men, knowing that from the Lord you will receive the reward of the inheritance; for you serve the Lord Christ."

Psalms 42:11

"Why are you cast down, O my soul? And why are you disquieted within me? Hope in God; for I shall yet praise Him, the help of my countenance and my God."

Romans 10:17

"So then faith comes by hearing,
and hearing by the word of God."

Psalms 118:23

"This was the LORD's doing;
It is marvelous in our eyes."

Psalms 1

Blessed is the man
Who walks not in the counsel of the ungodly,
Nor stands in the path of sinners,
Nor sits in the seat of the scornful;
But his delight is in the law of the LORD,

And in His law, he meditates day and night.
He shall be like a tree Planted by the rivers of water,
That brings forth its fruit in its season, whose leaf also shall not wither;
And whatever he does shall prosper.
The ungodly are not so,
But are like the chaff which the wind drives away.
Therefore, the ungodly shall not stand in the judgment,
Nor sinners in the congregation of the righteous.
For the LORD knows the way of the righteous,
But the way of the ungodly shall perish."

Hebrews 10:35
"Therefore, do not cast away your confidence, which has great reward."

Ephesians 4:26
"Be angry, and do not sin, do not let the sun go down on your wrath."

James 4:7
"Therefore, submit to God. Resist the devil and he will flee from you."

Psalms 23
The LORD is my shepherd; I shall not want.
He makes me to lie down in green pastures; He leads me beside the still waters.
He restores my soul;

He leads me in the paths of righteousness for His name's sake.

Yea, though I walk through the valley of the shadow of death,

I will fear no evil;

For You are with me; Your rod and Your staff, they comfort me.

You prepare a table before me in the presence of my enemies;

You anoint my head with oil; My cup runs over.

Surely goodness and mercy shall follow me
All the days of my life;
And I will dwell in the house of the LORD forever."

Psalm 37

Do not fret because of evildoers,
Nor be envious of the workers of iniquity.

For they shall soon be cut down like the grass, And wither as the green herb.
Trust in the Lord, and do good;
Dwell in the land, and feed on His faithfulness.

Delight yourself also in the Lord,
And He shall give you the desires of your heart.

[5] Commit your way to the Lord,
Trust also in Him,
And He shall bring it to pass.

He shall bring forth your righteousness as the light,
And your justice as the noonday.
Rest in the Lord, and wait patiently for Him;
Do not fret because of him who prospers in his way,
Because of the man who brings wicked schemes to pass.
Cease from anger, and forsake wrath; Do not fret— it only
causes harm.
For evildoers, shall be cut off;
But those who wait on the Lord, they shall inherit the earth.

[10] For yet a little while and the wicked shall be no more;
indeed, you will look carefully for his place, but it shall be
no more.
But the meek shall inherit the earth,
And shall delight themselves in the abundance of peace.
The wicked plots against the just,
And gnashes at him with his teeth.
The Lord laughs at him,
For He sees that his day is coming.

The wicked have drawn the sword and have bent their
bow, to cast down the poor and needy,
To slay those who are of upright conduct.

[15] Their sword shall enter their own heart,
And their bows shall be broken.

A little that a righteous man has
Is better than the riches of many wicked.

For the arms of the wicked shall be broken,
But the Lord upholds the righteous.

The Lord knows the days of the upright,
And their inheritance shall be forever.
They shall not be ashamed in the evil time,
And in the days of famine they shall be satisfied.

[20] But the wicked shall perish;
And the enemies of the Lord,
Like the splendor of the meadows, shall vanish.
Into smoke they shall vanish away.

The wicked borrows and does not repay,
But the righteous shows mercy and gives.

For those blessed by Him shall inherit the earth,
But those cursed by Him shall be cut off.

The steps of a good man are ordered by the Lord,
And He delights in his way.
Though he falls he shall not be utterly cast down;
For the Lord upholds him with His hand.
[25] I have been young, and now am old;
Yet I have not seen the righteous forsaken,
Nor his descendants begging bread.

He is ever merciful, and lends;
And his descendants are blessed.

Depart from evil, and do good;
And dwell forevermore.

For the Lord loves justice,
And does not forsake His saints;
They are preserved forever,
But the descendants of the wicked shall be cut off.

The righteous shall inherit the land,
And dwell in it forever.

[30] The mouth of the righteous speaks wisdom,
And his tongue talks of justice.

The law of his God is in his heart;
None of his steps shall slide.

The wicked watches the righteous,
And seeks to slay him.

The Lord will not leave him in his hand,
Nor condemn him when he is judged.
Wait on the Lord,
And keep His way,
And He shall exalt you to inherit the land;
When the wicked are cut off, you shall see it.

[35] I have seen the wicked in great power,
And spreading himself like a native green tree. Yet he
passed away, and behold, he was no more; indeed, I sought
him, but he could not be found.

Mark the blameless man, and observe the upright; for the future of that man is peace.

But the transgressors shall be destroyed together; the future of the wicked shall be cut off.

But the salvation of the righteous is from the Lord; He is their strength in the time of trouble.

[40] And the Lord shall help them and deliver them;
He shall deliver them from the wicked,
And save them,
Because they trust in Him."

Philippians 4:8
Meditate on These Things

"Finally, brethren, whatever things are true, whatever things are noble, whatever things are just, whatever things are pure, whatever things are lovely, whatever things are of good report, if there is any virtue and if there is anything praiseworthy— meditate on these things."

"My Go To Scriptures" are also available on E-Book as a FREE Gift! Go to the link below to download your copy today!

www.backtoeden.today

About the Author

Bettie, raised in Detroit, MI has been married for most of her life. First, as a pregnant teenager forced by her parents to marry. From the ages 19-27, the honor student's life took a sharp curve, down the road of an abusive marriage, illness, addictions, and prostitution.

Thank God, for March 13, 1979, the day that she surrendered to God, and cried out "What must I do to be saved from this wretched, low life?" JESUS was the answer, and still is!

Bettie's second and present marriage has also, surprisely had its share of disappointments, especially since they are both Christians. Adultery and brokenness have been a factor; but the Unconditional Love of God, Forgiveness and by applying the strategies, prayers and confessions found in this book, Ken and Bettie are daily living A Heavenly Marriage!!

As an author-minister, Bettie hopes that you, the reader will gain insight and instructions to avoid some of the pain that she experienced.

Presently, the Power Couple; Ken & Bettie Rusher enjoys quality time with their blended family. They also, love, love, love to travel, especially cruising.

Bettie is an entrepreneur, massage therapist, and ordained minister. She loves God and His Family, after all; we are one family under God!

For More Information-
Bettie J Rusher wants to hear from you!
For more information about Bettie's upcoming Volume Two & Three of the Heavenly Married Series & Create HIS Castle Webinars, or to find out how to book Bettie for your next event, contact Bettie @

www.scribesofeden.com www.kenbettie.com

Thanks, for submitting a positive review @ Amazon.com or where you purchased your book.

Hugs and Kisses!